D1459695

# NIGHT WITCHES

## *The Soviet Female Pilots Who Terrified the German Army*

# TABLE OF CONTENTS

# INTRODUCTION

The Night Witches were World War II's female volunteers who made one of the first all-female Night Bomber Regiments of the air forces in the Soviet Union. They were war heroines who participated in combat even though they didn't have any machine guns, radios, radars or parachutes. Yet, they used all of the advantages that a compass, map, pencils, and flashlight could possibly provide and helped to win the war.

Their missions slowed down the advancing German army during the four years of war. The number of their completed bombing raids was 30,000 in total, which is more than 23,000 tons of munitions. They used the darkness as their coverage and flew in biplanes that were often characterized as bare-boned plywood. They fought not only cruel Soviet winters in their poorly equipped planes but also sexual harassment and skepticism of their fellow male comrades. Nazis were terrified of Night Witches, and they even gave them this nickname (Nachthexen in German). It was due to their wooden plane's noises that reminded Germans of sweeping broomstick sounds.

Steve Prowse, the author of the "The Night Witches" screenplay said in one of his interviews that this "sweeping broom" sound was the only warning that Nazis had because these female air force squadrons were too small to appear on infrared locators and radar couldn't pick up their location either. Radio locators weren't useful either since Night Witches didn't use them, it was impossible to pick up the signal, which made them basically ghosts for the opposing army. Germans feared them and hated them so much that they awarded with Iron Cross medals any of their soldiers who would kill at least one Night Witch or down their planes.

Since they had impeccable strategies and fearless attacks, these pioneering Night Bomber Regiments, especially the 588th one that was later named the Night Witches, became one of the crucial assets for the Soviet Union and winning against the Nazis in World War II.

# Chapter 1:

# WORLD WAR II AND THE ROLE OF WOMEN IN THE SOVIET UNION

R ussian territory turned into a front-row battlefield after the Nazis started their invasion, which they named "Operation Barbarossa'.' That combat, in general, was reluctant in accepting female soldiers, but this acceptance was a product of necessity more than equality. The fact was that the Soviet Union expected from every able Soviet to fight and defend their homeland, and women were no exception. This was the first time that females served in the war's front lines. Furthermore, women excelled in many specialized duties, and all-female Soviet Fighter Pilot Regiments were the best example of this. The world had the opportunity to see the abilities and loyalty of Soviet women, and ultimately to witness their extraordinary achievements.

We can say that this warfare later impacted views on gender roles and women in all of the countries that nurtured Communism. Russia was the first of these countries that declared legal equality for women in 1917 and allowed them to serve in the military forces and participate in the war. This equality law referred to not only rights but also responsibilities for both male and female citizens. However, although Communist ideology relayed on social equality before anything else, this wasn't always exhibited in practice. At that time, the scope of women's affairs was still limited to traditional interests. Regardless of the universal military service law from 1925, war and military service was considered to be an exception from those interests; besides, even if the Soviet Union allowed females to enlist as volunteers, they were frequently dissuaded from service. Still, there was one government mission that was a keystone for later progress of feminism in the Union.

Russia's vital transportation system at the time was considered to be aviation. They anticipated that their air force would be especially important if the war starts. That is why the Soviet government prepared projects that would deal with this matter and trained all of the necessary air force crewmembers. This included pilots but also mechanics, navigators, and other support crew. Some historical sources say that the country made serious efforts to increase public awareness about the significance of transportation in such a vast country. Therefore, the government used different approaches to heighten citizen's enthusiasm for aviation.

Campaigns that had a purpose of heightening the public interest in aviation were successful, and subsequently, there were more and more people who volunteered to participate in all sorts of training. Thanks to these campaigns, the Soviet Union had many experts in mechanics, engineering, cartography, and geological surveying along with pilots as their main focus. The prime source for recruitment were university students, but this time not only men but female students too. Statistics say that the Red Army had approximately 400,000 women on the front lines during World War II and additional 800,000 female volunteers for other services for the battle. Some of these women were trained for combat, for the usage of automatic rifles or other light and heavy machine guns. It is said that there were almost 300,000 women who served in AA units that performed all sorts of activities, including firing the guns if necessary.

Even though the gender didn't limit women from obtaining skills to participate in combat, the Great Patriotic War had a different picture for them to fit in. They were expected to put an example of caring mothers who support brothers and husbands that fought to defend Mother Russia. Women were expected to stay home and nurture the children and exemplify the role of mother, wife, and sister rather than fight against the Nazis. During those years, even in Communism, there was the term "a good Russian woman" which means that she strives to fulfill her expected role while being a good communist that would do everything for her country as she would do for her own children.

# Chapter 2:

# FORMING AN ALL-FEMALE AIR FORCE REGIMENTS FOR THE WAR AGAINST THE NAZIS

A woman who was credited with forming all-female fighting squadrons was Marina Raskova. She was also known as the "Soviet Amelia Earhart" and not only because she was the first woman that ever navigated in the air force of Soviet Union but also because she had an impressive record of long-distance flights. Since she was already established in the Soviet Air Force, Raskova started receiving a large number of letters from women all across Russia and other countries of the Soviet Union. All of these women wanted to join their comrades in a war not only as support forces, but also as gunners or pilots. They wanted to be on the frontlines defending their homeland for various reasons. Some of them have lost their brothers or husbands, others have lost their friends and neighbors, but the point is – they didn't want to stand behind and watch their people die while Nazis ravage their homes or villages.

Marina Raskova saw an opportunity in these numerous requests and placed a petition for letting her form a fighting squadron that would have only female members. Soviet dictator Joseph Stalin approved the petition and in October 1941, gave the order to deploy three all-female units for the Soviet Union's Air Force. These three forces weren't only for flying missions, but for fighting back. This act of deploying air force squadrons and allowing them to engage in combat made the Soviet Union the first nation to ever approve this kind of right to women. Before that, females could only help with the transportation of ammunition or planes and the men took over afterward, so this was the first time that women could actually fight.

After it was officially approved, Raskova immediately started forming teams. Even though there were more than 2,000 applicants, she had to select approximately 400 women for all of the units. Most of the females that ended up being a part of three squadrons were young students (17-26 years old), and they all moved to a small town named Engels. This city was located north of Stalingrad and was the home of the Angels School of Aviation that provided training for all 400 members of the Soviet Air Force. The education in Engels was highly compressed since they had to learn everything that other soldiers studied for several years in just a few months. Every member of the future all-female squadron underwent training in piloting, navigating, and maintenance of the plane along with performing as members of the ground crew.

Regardless of their efforts and capabilities, all of these women faced many difficulties because most of the men in military personnel didn't believe that females could add value when it comes to combat. Since Raskova was already familiar with the soldiers' mindset, she tried to prepare her fellow squadron members for these kinds of attitudes. Many of them had to deal with sexual harassment during training and grueling conditions just because they were women. The main issue was that men thought that going to the front lines was their thing and that fighting wasn't for "little girls" as they used to call them.

The Soviet military wasn't prepared for women pilots at the time. Also, they weren't exactly thrilled about the idea of having them at the frontlines, so they offered these three female squadrons' poor resources. Women who were flyers received male uniforms that were handed down from other soldiers. Even boots were oversized, so they often had to stuff them with bedding just to be able to walk properly.

The equipment they received for combat wasn't much better. They got Polikarpov Po2 biplanes that were outdated. Additionally, the military provided them with crop-dusters from the 1920s that were used for training before that. These planes, in general, were never meant for combat since they had opened cockpits and two-seaters. These planes were also known as the "coffins with wings" among the soldiers. Furthermore, these aircraft didn't have almost any protection from its elements. They were basically made of plywood with canvas, which was pulled over. Another thing that made things even worse is that these planes were almost impossible to fly at night because the pilots had to endure harsh temperatures of Soviet winters. It is said that temperatures were sometimes so low that bare skin would ripen off just by touching the cold plane.

Planes that female squadrons were supposed to pilot had a limited weight capacity. The military also declared that due to the limited funds, they couldn't provide other items needed for combat. On the other hand, their male comrades had more luck, thus more equipment. As we already mentioned, they didn't have "luxury" of using parachutes, guns, radios or radars. Contrarily, they had to turn to use so-called rudimentary tools. This included flashlights, pencils, stopwatches, rulers, compasses, and maps.

Although things looked really bad when the equipment was distributed, there were some advantages of these old aircraft that these strong women used to their advantage in combat. The thing was that the maximum speed of Po2's and crop-dusters that female squadrons used were slower than the stall speed of any Nazi plane. Ironically, this meant that wooden planes could maneuver faster than the enemy. Therefore, slower old planes turned out to be hard to target and useful to attack with. One additional advantage was the fact that these initially non-combat planes could take off easily from most locations. The same thing applies when it comes to landing too.

However, there were some serious downsides. Firstly, these aircraft couldn't carry defense ammunition. If they came under the enemy fires, pilots had to dive their planes and try to avoid the attack. Nazi tracer bullets had a pyrotechnical charge. If they managed to hit wooden aircraft, it would just burst into flames. And if we take into consideration that Soviet female pilots didn't have parachutes, their chance of survival was minimal.

World War II empowered nationalism that was already strong in Russia. This was one of the main reasons why Russian women wanted to be a part of the military and serve their country. Communistic ideology promoted patriotism, but rather than questioning what women could do to help fight against the occupation of their homeland, and many asked why they would do that? One of the most quoted answers to this question was taken from AA's gunner Tikhonovich. When she was asked why she wanted to volunteer in combat and perform activities that were considered to be "unwomanly" and dangerous, she answered "'Motherland,' and we meant the same thing for us."

# Chapter 3:

# HOW NIGHT WITCHES GOT THEIR NAMES

We already said that the Night Witches were a unique example of female combatants. Other countries like the United States allowed women to be members of plane crews and fly even in their early forces. However, all of them were limited to support roles. This is where Stalin came in, being the first to allow females to engage in combat. They were the first women in a war that could return fire, fly planes, and drop bombs on the enemy lines.

Poor aircraft that the Soviet government gave their female combatants turned out to help them gain a nickname that was widely recognized. The gliding technique that Raskova and her female comrades used reminded Nazis of witches' broomsticks.

That is why Germans called them "Nachthexen" or Night Witches. It is said that the Nazi troops were so terrified of these Soviet stealth attackers that they didn't want to smoke during the night. They believed that the light of the cigarette could reveal their position to the "Nachthexen." The 588th Regiment squadron heard about the nickname that the Nazis gave them, and adopted it as a badge of pride, thus used it in further battle.

There was a rumor that the Night Witches used experimental medicines, which gave them some kind of feline night vision. These rumors were mostly spread by the Soviet government. The purpose of these rumors was to increase fear among Germans who were already in awe of "Nachthexen" skills. When Nazis heard that the Soviets supposedly had air force members with enhanced night vision, they automatically responded by issuing a prestigious medal for those who manage to shoot a Night Witch. This medal was named "Iron Cross," and any German could obtain it as long as he was able to shoot down at least one of the Night Witches' aircraft or members.

On the other hand, the Night Witches were aware of their technical disadvantages. That is why they always flew during the night. Their strategy was simple - they always flew in groups of three. Two planes were decoys. They were supposed to draw the attention of German gunfire and searchlights while the third plane went toward the target and dropped the bombs. These two decoys would later go off in opposite directions. They avoided gunshots by wildly twisting the aircraft afterward.

This action was repeated until all of the bombs were dropped.

The key point of this strategy was the slow speed of Night Witches' planes. It provided them with better maneuverability because the Nazis had a very small amount of time to return the fire. The main reason for this was a difference in speed. Also, the Nazis' planes had to make wide turns before being able to return fire again. This was advantageous for the Night Witches to escape into the night. Furthermore, lack of radio signals and primitive construction of the Soviet aircraft made Night Witches almost impossible to detect so Germans couldn't track them.

Still, not all members of the all-female air force escaped. During the four years of combat, the Night Witches lost 32 pilots in total. One of them was their Colonel Raskova who died fighting at the frontline. She was buried in the Kremlin with all of the state's honors while 23 pilots of her squadron received "Hero of the Soviet Union" titles.

Still, all of these female combat participants were excluded from the official parade in Moscow. Many contemporary historians and feminists find this controversial. According to the historical sources, when the victory - day parade in Moscow came, the government stated that the planes of the Night Witches were too slow. Thus, there was no need for them to participate in the parade.

Still, the name of the Night Witches was always associated with courage and incredible skill. These females used every chance to celebrate their womanhood. Although they had to face many obstacles, they decided to point out their achievements as females. Coloring their lips with navigational pencils and drawing flowers on their planes was one way to do that. Even the enemy wasn't able to deny the significant role that "Nichthexen" played in the war. Their skills helped manifest some of the most remarkable achievements in the history of aerial combat.

# Chapter 4:

# NIGHT WITCHES AS PATRIOTS AND FEMINIST INSPIRATION

We return once more to the reasons for entering the military in the first place. Most of these women had two reasons: fulfilling an ambition or personal reasons such a family member loss. For example, one of the 588th Night Bombers Regiment named Nadezhda Popova wanted a position on the frontline because she wanted revenge. Her brother was killed in battle. Another example is one of the fighting aces named Lidiya Litvyak that wanted redemption for her family if she could prove herself by being good in air combat. Litvyak's father was condemned and killed along with thousands of other prisoners for undisclosed reasons. Since he was considered to be an "enemy of the people" she wanted to erase that kind of image for her father by participating in combat.

Another example of patriotism can be found in a letter written by Ekaterina Budanova. She wrote to her sister, saying that she wanted to devote her life to fighting against the Nazis. She said that she was not afraid to give her life and if she were "fated to perish" it would "cost the enemy dearly." She also wrote about her aircraft named "Yak," and she said that her life is connected to it and if necessary, they would both die like heroes. Budanova died in 1943, but before that, she was already considered to be a "fighter ace," and she had six independent skills in combat reported. She was killed in action and died in a skirmish taking down three German Messerschmitt aircraft with her.

Young Communists were prepared for war by organizations specialized for combat skills and flight training. Chemical and defense warfare was determined by the military too. The Soviet Society for Cooperation in Defense and Aviation-Chemical Development named "The Osoaviakhim" was a paramilitary organization. It was founded in 1927, and its main purpose was to provide necessary training of all sorts. By the year of 1935, this organization had developed a network that had more than 150 air-clubs that could train pilots. During these several years, women also applied for training. The government stated that officially, every young woman in the Soviet Union was encouraged to apply and participate in Osoaviakhim training. Still, women most frequently faced obstacles whenever they tried to get into the organization and participate in flight training. One of the many who faced the opposition of allowing women into flight training was Marina Checheneva. She was later awarded the prestigious title, becoming the "Hero of the Soviet Union" as a member of the Night Bomber pilot service. She said that the organization often stated that aviation was not suitable for women and that they used all kinds of reasons to dissuade them from joining the air clubs.

Valentine Pavlovna wanted to avenge the death of her father, so she sought military service. However, when she requested that one of her combat assignments was to shoot, the organization denied her request. They advised her to work as a phone operator because that was the "most vital work" that she could be qualified for. Unfortunately, these weren't single-cased scenarios. These kinds of reasons were actually quite common. Whenever some young woman requested special training, they were denied. It is said that Pavlovna was so revolted by the response that she got, she replied to this chauvinist reasoning by saying that phone receivers don't shoot; thus, she couldn't use them.

Contrarily, Marina Raskova didn't have any tragic reason to become a pilot. She was one of the young Soviet women who wanted to pursue her ambitions. In childhood, she led a very different life and was schooled to become an opera singer. Unfortunately, she became ill when she turned fifteen, so she had to look for another path in life. She chose to study engineering, chemistry, and navigation and not only did she have high education, but she became the first woman that had ever earned a professional air navigator diploma in USSR (1934). She even gained the position of instructor at Zhukovsky Air Force Engineering Academy that was located in Moscow. According to the historical records, the Academy was the first place in which she faced direct discrimination from other officers who were her male colleagues. However, she was so skilled, and her performance was so impeccable that all of the male students changed their opinions. After this, Raskova was sent by the Academy to Central Flying club to flight instruction, also in Moscow. She obtained her pilot's license just one year after she officially became a navigator and she started to fly independently before the beginning of 1935.

In the next three years, Raskova became known widely for establishing world records in non-stop flights over long distances. That is where her previously used nickname "Soviet Amelia Earhart" came from. Her piloting achievements were deemed equal to Earhart's. One of the most representative examples is her 6,000 km flight from Moscow to Rodina, which is a city located in the Soviet Far East. Raskova didn't fly alone, and the interesting fact is that both of her co-pilots were also women. Their names were Paulina Osipenko and Valentina Grizodubova. These three pilots were the first ones that received one of the most prestigious titles of that time becoming Heroes of the Soviet Union.

Marina Raskova was undoubtedly one of the most inspirational characters for many other women to join the air force during this period. The interest in aviation was so big that by the end of the 1930s the number of USSR's trained female pilots was accounted to be approximately one-third of the total number of pilots in the Union. And when the war emerged in 1941, many of these women wrote to Raskova asking her to join the war and use their flight skills to fight against the occupation of the Nazis. Most of these letters were referring to finding a way to go to the frontline, and an air force if possible.

Since Raskova was already quite influential at the time, she decided to use her position on the People's Defense Committee and persuaded Stalin to approve the formation of all-female aviation combat regiments. It is said that Stalin, in general, had an interest in the potential of female pilots and how he could use them in international propaganda. That is why he granted Raskova's request in 1941 and allowed her to select candidates for the all-female air force group. This group was initially named 122nd Composite Air Group, but it was later reorganized as three regiments: the 586th Fighter Aviation Regiment, the 587th Day

Bomber Aviation Regiment, and the 588th Night Bomber Aviation Regiment.

All of the candidates that Raskova selected were divided into four categories. They were based on candidates' backgrounds and skills. The final division of the categories was the following: a group of pilots, a group of mechanics, a group of navigators and a group of armories. Most of these women were students who had certain technical skills and knowledge, but there were also some of those who underwent Osoaviakhim training before the war began. Whether they were candidates for bomber pilots or fighters, they all had to have at least 500 flying hours of training. This requirement was a high standard, and all of the regular members spent at least three years of intensive training to acquire it. However, Raskova's female candidates didn't have the luxury of time, so they had to finish 500 flying hours in only a few months.

Their training was divided into ten courses per day. Additionally, they had two drilling hours daily, and navigators had it even harder. Among all of these courses and drilling hours, they had to study the Morse code. This resulted in extended schedules and a sleep rate of under 5 hours at night during the whole training. Raskova wanted to produce highly skilled female pilots. She requested superb performances from all of her candidates, so it wasn't unusual for her to surprise them with night drills. She was very harsh because she wanted to prepare them for the horrific conditions that would await them on the frontline. All of the pilots that later formed a 588th Bomber Regiment had a task to fly during the night and wreak havoc on the Nazis' army. The average time of flights expected from each aircraft was 15 per night.

Let's recall that all of these regiments flew using Po2 planes, which weren't meant for combat. These were mostly training planes that had bomb racks. They had no weapons except light machine guns and the stealth of the aircraft, which was a product of flare mufflers.

The planes could carry up to 300kg of bombs if the bombs were strapped to the aircraft's wings. The pilots of the 588th regiment used their Po2 planes to bomb bridges or supplies of the most heavily guarded parts of the German troops. Most of these fortified places had anti-aircraft guns, but the main purpose of the 588th Bomber Regiment was to provoke and maintain chaos, which will prevent Nazis from sleeping, making them stay in a constant state of alert and keeping them additionally stressed every night.

As we already mentioned, Po2s never flew alone. There were always two planes that would act as decoys and draw attention while the one plane that was under stealth approaches bombing the Germans. The idea was that the bombing plane always flew over the target without producing any sound and dropped the intended bombs before the enemy even noticed its presence. All of the ladies that participated in these night bombing missions took pride in their actions of relentless harassment of the Nazis. One of the pilots, Nadezhda Popova, said in one of her interviews that there was even a rumor that all members of the female air force received injections with supernatural powers. Along with the rumors of experimental medicines, this added even more mystery to the Soviet female Regiments.

The "Nachthexen" became nocturnal bombers that were feared and respected for their skills even though they faced so many difficulties just because they were women. Marina Raskova, the Colonel of the Regiment, wasn't only respected by the pilots she trained and flew with, but by all military peers in the Soviet Air Force. She was described as a driven leader and one of the most skilled pilots in the world. Along with her other qualities, she was considered to be one of the greatest inspirations to young Russian women in the years to come. The idea of a young, beautiful, and talented woman that pursued her ambition and fought for her place among the all-male comrades was highly motivational. Also, being the commander of three full female regiments and providing females the possibility of fighting on the frontline for the first time ever was one of the biggest achievements for gender equality in the era of Communism.

# NIGHT WITCHES AND THEIR SIGNIFICANCE IN PERCEPTION OF COMBAT ELIGIBILITY DURING AND AFTER WORLD WAR II

Although they were trained to be professional pilots with excessive combat skills, many women dealt with conflict feelings, which were the product of both excitement and anxiety. On the one hand, they wanted to prove that their skills were good enough for fighting and for air combat. On the other hand, it was hard for them to adjust to this new role that they were given in the warfare.

One of the pilots from the 587th Regiment named Mariya Dolina talked about her inner conflict. She said that she wanted to fight for the freedom of her people, but she never wanted to kill. For her, the dream was to be one of the girls that helped liberate her land but fighting to kill was something that she had to process along the way. Dolina was one of the pilots that successfully accomplished more than 200 combat missions during the war and flew over 2,800 hours as a member of the 587th Bombing Regiment.

Nadezhda Popova that we already mentioned several times was a pilot in the 588th – The Night Witch Bombing Regiment. As she recalled in one of her statements, her first combat mission was a battlefield in Ukraine. She said that she remembered that at first, everything was pitch black and that she regained her sight once she flew further up in the air. According to her, the Ukrainian frontline had different colored tracer lights that were moving through the dark sky. Popova, like all other pilots, was trained to search for these tracer lights along with learning how to pilot in total darkness. For her, that was also the first time to witness the real horror of war and fatal descent of her comrades' aircraft. She continued with her mission and successfully dropped the bombs on the intended targets.

One of the hardest things not only for female pilots but all those who fought, in general, was thinking about everything that they saw during the war. As far as the Night Witches were concerned, their best strategy was to fly as many missions as possible and keep their minds off it. They all focused on work as much as possible to avoid thinking about death. This was one of the reasons why they had many successive flights every night during the war. They sometimes flew up to 18 missions per night. Nadezhda Popova, in particular, was one of the pilots who accomplished this number of missions in one single winter night when the Soviet forces fought in Poland.

All of the ladies that fought in the Soviet Air Force were conscious that they had to prove themselves constantly. On the one hand, as pilots to their fellow men fighters, and on the other, they had to prove to Russia that they were deserving patriots. To be able to do that, they had to "meet or even surpass the standards set by male aviators'.' It was no secret that men in the air force frequently undermined their skills and judged them most of the time. However, this kind of attitude didn't discourage them. On the contrary, that is why they tried even harder to hone their flight and combat skills.

Although formally, they had the same rights, there was a double standard for male and female soldiers that underwent the same training and had the same skills. There was a double standard, even for the jobs that both genders were performing based on the previously mentioned criteria. Conflict emerged because there was confusion about this dual role of females–being a woman and a fighter at the same time. The conflict was mostly a product of different expectations for both of these roles. It wasn't uncommon for men to declare that they were repulsed by women who weren't gentle and feminine because, according to them, women weren't supposed to act tough. However, they didn't value women who couldn't perform any task perfectly.

Another case of difficult situations that female pilots had to deal with was a girl who volunteered to become a member of the firing squad that executed deserters. After she joined, all of her fellow squad members refused to talk to her. This kind of treatment was additional emotional stress, and when this girl had a post-war psychiatric treatment, she faced insensitivity once again. In fact, she was told that she should get married and have many children if she wanted to get better and get her soul back. It was very common that people didn't really support the policy of allowing women to be a part of the military forces. These people often acted paranoid and poorly treated all of the females who participated in war activities.

Some would argue that harmless flirtation was a mechanism of coping for young female fighters. It is said that they saw it as a nice distraction from death and destruction that they had to witness every day. Even though Night Witches were a sort of killing machine, they were human beings, young girls above all other things. They used to wear makeup even if the military prohibited it. Their attitude was that even though their youth came during the war, they could have it only once. Since they worked along with their male colleagues to defend their homes from occupation, these kinds of interactions created a social environment that wasn't ordinary for that era. Social norms were different, almost blurred. Since all of them were constantly on the verge of death, things were different.

There is an example of a female soldier that said that many of those who were fighting on the frontline lived in severe conditions. They were starving, spent days or sometimes even weeks without bathing. Not to mention the fact that they were constantly exhausted from the battle. According to her, this wasn't exactly an environment for any physical relationship. She said that many thought that women on the front line had a lot of relationships. Most of the people even considered them "easy," but the truth was that they didn't have much time to think about that stuff. They were busy trying to survive.

Later, when these women showed that they had what it took to be on the battlefield and exhibited their skills, gender became an irrelevant label. The do-or-die instinct became something necessary because surviving was the only goal along with the country's defense. It is not a surprise that harsh conditions on the battlefield formed many lifetime friendships. Their dedication was tested in extreme conditions, and since both women and men could die at any moment, their connections during the warfare were even closer and more profound. One of the 125th Guards Bomber Regiment members, Anna Kirilina – an armament mechanic said that as a woman, she felt constantly physically overstrained because that's what wartime does. She didn't consider that war was a place for women, or for anyone. However, she explained that all of those battles blessed her not with friends but with relatives, brothers, and sisters that she shared so much with. She added that four years of peaceful life couldn't be compared to four years on the frontline and that the amount of experience that you share with others in those circumstances leaves a connection that lasts forever.

The change of view about another gender during combat wasn't only referring to men viewing women. Female war participants also had the opportunity to see another side of male characters that they might have never seen if things were different. Some female soldiers gained a new kind of respect for their comrades. They had the opportunity to share many different and difficult situations, to see their weaknesses and their strengths, to help them fight their fears and cope with similar burdens. All of these things connected fellow soldiers of both genders on a deeper level. Regardless of being a man or a woman, they had seen each other cry, been terrified or upset if they had to kill or witness the killing. They shared all of these situations as companions and equals, which had a great impact on the overall impression on all of them after the war ended.

All of the pilots, including the Night Witches, considered protecting their comrades from being one of the most important segments of defense along with their missions. They never separated men from women because, as they said, "war doesn't spare anyone" and it made no difference either between sex and age. The brutality of war and the difficulty of its acceptance forced women to focus on their tasks fully. Firstly, they had to deal with the initial shock, then to adapt to the fact that with each mission they entered a "who will win'?' kind of situation. They had to accept that it was life or death all the time and they couldn't choose. It was simple - Nazis were destroying them, they were destroying Nazis, and that was what war was all about.

Female air-force squadrons faced a big change when the Great Patriotic War ended in 1945, and they were demobilized. It was a great shock because they had spent years acquiring the skills and the knowledge that was necessary for military services during the war. They faced many enemies and challenged many rules to become competent air combat pilots and serve their country. They had proven themselves in combat, and many of them survived not only social skepticism during the whole time but also the numerous life-threatening missions that helped the Soviet Union win against the Germans. But when the war ended, they were automatically discharged not only from their military service but banned from academies, which were the only relevant organizations for becoming an officer or a pilot in the USSR. The truth was that the government wanted to discourage all of the female survivors from continuing their careers in the military. They didn't even want them to have a job in some related positions.

The government had a plan to recover Russia after the war, and that plan didn't include women as a part of military force but counted them as a source of labor that was essential for civilians. All of the surviving members of the fearless Night Witches ended up banned from the army. They were told to return to their homes because the country didn't need them as pilots or soldiers anymore. They were told to start families and pursue careers as a part of the civilian workforce.

The fact was that war left the country in destruction. But the Soviet government promoted women as mothers and wives before everything else. After the war, they became workers too, and by the end of 1945, women represented around 63% of the total workforce in Moscow. The self-sacrificing role of women for her family and mostly for Mother Russia was strongly emphasized and even publicly enforced. Still, the Night Witches were practically denied the possibility of having a further career in both military and aviation, and they were put under social pressure to accept the importance of the family as the highest post-war priority. The primary post-war goal of the nation was to be rebuilt, and every citizen had to make sure that their actions were focused on meeting that goal.

The new Soviet country didn't have a place for women who were pilots and military officers that served in the war. That image was outweighed by a new Soviet woman who was supposed to be a loving wife and mother, and one of the pillars of post-war society. This meant that, in essence, all of the sacrifices and efforts that all members of the Night Witches made during the four years of war were basically deleted as insignificant.

Some of the Night Witches peacefully accepted the fact that their combat skills weren't needed once the war ended. Irina Rakobolskaya, another pilot of the 588th Bombing Regiment, said that she needed to rationalize the reality. She said that for her, it was a challenge pursuing a piloting career and having a family even before she went to war. According to her, it was justified to have women in combat because the country's freedom was in danger, and its defense was the whole nation's top priority. But when the war ended and peaceful days started women's only reason to fly was for sports. Rakobolskaya declared that there wasn't any other reason for women to pilot after the war and that they should all try to combine their careers with motherhood and family.

Most of the pilots in the all-female Air Forces were young. It wasn't a surprise that many of them had an alternative occupation if they hadn't made it into aviation. Since most of them attended university before World War II began, they returned to finish schooling once when the war was over.

Contrarily, some women attempted staying in aviation after the war, but they couldn't fly mostly because they had post-traumatic stress or all sorts of physical injuries. The main reason for bad health, both physical and mental, was a lack of decent living conditions on the battlefront and long periods of exhaustion and malnutrition. Even if they tried to fly in civil aviation, there were many of them who couldn't pass the medical examinations.

Even those members of the Night Witches who had wed military husbands had difficulties in post-war life. The social hypocrisy was hard to deal with even though the society always expected that the woman should defer to the career of her husband and lead a more domestic life. Some of the Night Witches wanted to continue their aviation careers despite the obstacles they had to deal with. One of these examples is Ekaterina Raibova, who went to Zhukovsky Militar Aviation Academy after the war and looked for employment. But her commanding officer had an answer that was different from what she expected. He told her that she had already proved what she was capable of when her country needed help, but that country didn't need that help anymore. He added that military studies were too hard for a woman because they can take a heavy toll on such a fragile body and that she already lost her health and her strength in war. He denied her request for enrolling in Military Academy by saying that it was for her own protection and that she should study something in the civilian university. Even though the commanding officer of Zhukovsky Militar Aviation Academy wanted to dissuade Riabova from entering the academy that once again became "only male" territory, she finished her studies, started a family and worked on many engagements in Asia and Europe.

Even though the policy towards the women in the army changed after the war, it was a fact that female volunteers for military service made up approximately 8% of the total combat Soviet forces during the battle. All of these women proved on the frontline that gender doesn't matter when it comes to skills. We would point out that 91

Russian women received awards of the highest value – the Hero of the Soviet Union medals. Additionally, 150, 000 women were decorated and honored for their war achievements too. When it came to the "Hero of the Soviet Union medal" it is important to know that 30 were awarded to the members of the Night Witches. The other two regiments lost at least 50 other female members honored with this medal, and they were later entitled "the Guards'.'

One of the events that influenced the Night Witches heavily during the war was the death of their Colonel Marina Raskova, who died on the 4th of January in 1943, as we previously mentioned. She piloted a Po2 plane during the heavy snowstorm on the road to the Stalingrad's front and died along with her 4 regiment comrades who were flying along with her. Her formation was crushed near the Volga, and there were no survivors. When Raskova died, 587th Regiment got a new Colonel. His name was Valentin Markov. According to Markov's words, he didn't know how to react at first or what to expect from the squad. It was difficult to imagine taking leadership over such an un-precedent unit. Still, his goal was to act strict and just, as he would act in front of any other member. It didn't take much time for him to realize that when it came to combat skills, there were no differences even though the regiment members were all female.

Markov pointed out that their performance was remarkable and that the main reason for that was their devotion to duty and hard training that they did. He added that they respected the fact that he was treating them as equals and that they never complained. He even said that in the end, it became more comfortable for him to lead a female regiment rather than the male one. This regiment, as we already said, got the elite status of "Guards." They were later reorganized, and their regiment got a new name. Along the 558th Night Witches, the Soviet Union had the 125th Guards Bomber Regiment. The new name of the regiment was given in honor of their fallen Colonel and leader Marina Raskova.

Even after she died, Raskova remained to be a strong inspiration to all of the air force crew that she trained. Members of all three female regiments kept following her advice and performed their duties as pilots, technicians, and navigators with integrity. It is said that many women carried Raskova's photo in their suits during their missions as a token of good luck. One of the Night Witch's navigators Galina Brok-Beltsova said that they had a nickname that was used only among the female regiments. They called themselves ''Raskovi'' which meant that they were ''children'' of Raskova. She inspired them to be brave and to make sure that her effort in promoting aviation and providing an opportunity for Russian girls to fight among men like equals wasn't in vain. They wanted to preserve her legacy.

The defense of Mother Russia's soil brought all classes together, no matter the gender or any other characteristics that would be important otherwise. Still, what Raskova and her Night Witches did for the country was far more important than just provoking the rumor about being the supernatural nocturnal beings or ''Nachthexen''. They used the most rudiment equipment such as Polikarpovs that could carry no more than two bombs at the time and performed over 30 000 successful maneuvers. To make an even stronger impact on the German troops, Night Witches sometimes sent out 40 crews (2 people each) for one night. Every time the plane dropped the bombs, it had to return to re-arm and since the weight of the bombs forced Po2s to be on the lower altitudes all of the missions had to be done during the night. And the most successful pilots in performing one of the most difficult missions such as these were the members of the 588th Bomber Regiment, thus the Night Witches. It is said that they had 12 commandments and that the first one was "Be proud that you are a woman".

# Chapter 5:

# ADDITIONAL DIFFICULTIES THAT NIGHT WITCHES HAD TO FACE DURING COMBAT

One of the most impressive names from the all-female air force regiment was Yekaterina Budanova and a fighter pilot that we already mentioned Lydia Litvyak. They were both pronounced the only female fighter aces in the world, and they were credited for over 25 solo kills in total. Litvyak was otherwise known as the "White Rose of Stalingrad" because, according to the stories, she always had white flowers painted on her aircraft. Both of these fearsome ladies were elite pilots or free hunters, and they prowled enemy planes with such precision that the Nazi pilots would try to flee as soon as they spotted them on the battlefield.

Raskova's Dive Bomber Regiments were facing a lot of difficulties. Pilots were skeptical about the ability of airwoman to handle airplanes such as Po2, which were considered to be highly demanding in both mental and physical aspects. Po2 was a twin-tailed; high tech plane of the time and even the strongest and the most skilled among the male pilots had difficulties with the control stick to get the aircraft off the ground. The additional concern was those female pilots wouldn't have enough strength to control the plane while recharging the machine gun that needed at least 60kg of force to be used. Still, during the war, some of the Raskova's Guard members had the opportunity to fly Po2s, and they performed so well that five of them were honored with the highest USSR awards.

On the other hand, there were the Night Witches who were flying antique, small wooden biplanes. Equipped with nothing but pencils, compasses, maps, rulers, and flashlights they weren't exactly the best when it came to laps. However, they were one of the most successful Soviet air force units when it came to producing heroes. One of the POW's said that whenever Night Witches bombed their troops there was a line at the radio station that said "Attention, attention, the ladies are in the air, stay in your shelter'". One of the Night Witches' mechanics Nina Yegorova said that Germans liked to sleep at night and that her Bombing Regiment didn't make their life easier because they disturbed German troops' sleep during the whole night. She said that the pilots could hear Nazis screaming "Nachthexen" while they were gliding over their targets.

Although in the beginning, the three women's regiments faced many obstacles and survived different forms of harassment, they were given missions that were similar to male regiments. There was no safety restriction, and they went to the front ending up with more stories than all of the other male squadrons.

One of the actions of the 586th Bombing Regiment saved many lives and a whole train station at one point. Tamara Pamyatnykh and Raisa Surnachevskaya, two pilots, intercepted a German communication and went to stop two enemy planes. However, due to the miscommunication of the German crew, they ended up seeing 42 enemy aircrafts approaching the station full of trains and people. The two brave pilots immediately contacted their commander asking for instructions and order to attack. The strategy that they used was the following: they dived two times through the German formation. Both of them shot one Nazi bomber each time they passed. With this strategy, they forced the rest of the bombers to drop their ammunition on the fields close to the station but save the trains and the people. Unfortunately, the Pamyatnyhk was hit during the attack, but she survived. She recalled this experience as one of the most dramatic ones in her life. According to her, she was falling at high speed and unable to open the belt. When she was finally able to remove the belt, it was too late to jump, but she was thrown down from her cockpit. She managed to land without any fatal wounds, but when she saw her fellow pilot Raisa landing another attack on Germans alone, so she was more concerned for her survival. But they both managed to survive the war and Surnchevskaya was considered to be the only combat pilot that ever flew while being pregnant.

It was highly unlikely that all of these stories would end without casualties. During the Soviet fights in World War II, the Eastern Front was one of the most dangerous fronts of all. Still, the female air force groups were in the thick of the battlefield. 588th Bombing Regiment suffered huge losses due to its fragile aircraft, which were highly flammable.

There were more tragic reasons why some women headed to combat at all costs. A pilot named Yevdokiya Nosal had one of those reasons. Her baby was killed during the hospital bombing just a few hours after she delivered. Even though Nosal was unharmed, she looked for vengeance. That was the main reason that she later joined the female air-force regiments and flew as many missions as possible every night. She was declared to be one of the best Guard's pilots but died of a headshot in combat. Since she commanded a Po2 aircraft that had dual controls (due to the fact it was designed for training), Nosal's navigator had to fly the plane back to the base while holding up the dead body of her colleague.

Everyone interested in Night Witches should be able to see a lot of differences and similarities between the female experiences in the USSSR at that period and some experiences that western women faced in other fields. The truth is that despite the fact that the Soviet Union was built on the foundation of Bolshevism, and that Stalin turned it to the right in an extreme way, it was still obvious that the USSR was more progressive than the West when it came to the presence of women in the workforce sectors. We already talked about the reactions that the Night Witches faced when they applied for pilot training. But that wasn't the only thing that tried to stop them. Many parents were against their daughters becoming pilots. Bondareva, one of the 46th Regiment pilots said that her father was against it from the beginning. Since all of her family members were traditionally steelworkers, she said that her father believed that she could easily become a steelworker rather than a pilot.

In the beginning, Soviet female pilots were often belittled. The first time when the regiments arrived at the front one of the division commanders said that he didn't receive fighters but "12 little princesses" complaining that he didn't know what to do with them. Their male comrades were also cruel and frequently rejected female rookies to fly with them as wingmen. Supposedly, they wanted to protect the "weaker ones," but the real reason was that they didn't want to give them a chance to fly with pilot veterans.

When Raskova brought a male instructor to teach her candidates dive-bombing for the first time, he refused because he thought it was ridiculous even to consider the possibility of women learning how to dive-bomb. Still, Raskova was persistent, and once that the instructor saw how capable his "ridiculous" pilots were, he immediately had to take his words back. One of the most notable characteristics of the Night Witches and their fellow regiments during their air-force work was that they never had special treatment because they were women.

Valentin Markov, the Colonel who replaced Raskova and led the female regiments, noted that even his superiors didn't make any distinction between the units on a gender basis and that the girls were very proud of that fact. Although they had poor treatment at the beginning, later in the war airwomen received the same mission types, served in the same divisions as men and even had the same uniforms (even the underwear was the same). One of the examples that Russians took the strength of their women pilots for granted was the difference between the Night Witches and American WASP when it comes to some basic rules. For instance, Russian girls never had any physical help, not even when they carried 100kg heavy bombs. Contrarily, there was a regulation that forbade American WASPs to fly if they had their periods.

Still, the women of the all three Soviet Air Force regiment were proud of their gender, and they often used slogans that celebrated their womanhood. The Night Witches along with other two Guard regiments, valued their all-female units and worked hard to keep them. One of the historians that researched the Night Witches phenomenon, Reina Pennington, sad that there was a conversation between the commander of the front – Rokossovskii and air force army commander Vershinin that best described the importance of there being all-female regiments to the girls. It all started with Rokossovskii, who was concerned that the women couldn't do everything by themselves and that they should send at least 20 men to help them with all kinds of work. This proposition provoked rebellion by the girls who said that they could do everything on their own. We can say that this relationship between female pride and their unspoken agreement that it was only normal that women could fight the same as men, is quite interesting.

One of the typical Communist opinions regarding this topic was given by Alexandra Akimova, one of the Night Witches' navigators. She said that the core of female nature is against the idea of combat because all women have a maternal instinct, which means that it is in their nature to want to give birth to children and nurture them. According to her, women in the military are not a natural event but a product of need. She thought that American women didn't realize this and that they had some romantic ideas about serving in army forces, making them want to become a part of it. Akimova explained this quite straightforwardly by saying that American women didn't really know or understand the true horrifying nature of war and that if all of the world's women united, the war would be an impossible thing to happen in the first place. This was a common opinion among the USSR's airwomen; still one of the commanders from the 586 Bomber Regiment-Kladiya Pankratova, didn't share their opinion.

She believed that both women and men can be pilots in military forces and that they can both complete any combat mission, especially when a misfortune such as war befalls their homeland. But then the war ended, and men weren't forced to retire, but she stated that she was forced to.

After the war ended, almost all of the surviving female air force members were banned from flying. But there were just a few of those who shared the revolt of Pankratova to this kind of post-war treatment. Most of the other women combatants turned to their lives as civilians leaving the military behind.

When it comes to individual cases, some didn't want to look too feminine when they became pilots and, on the contrary, some were proud of their womanhood. Tatiana Makarova was one of those girls who adopted some of the attitudes that were mostly masculine since she was raised in a traditional family. It is said that she always tried to cover up her feminine side and that she was ashamed to appear in front of other aviators if she didn't at least talk in a rude tone to others. However, most of these three regiment members, especially the Night Witches were unashamedly girlish, and one of their best presenters was the "White Rose of Stalingrad" who has already appeared several times through the text of this book. All of her fellow pilots considered her to be a perfect example of what a charmed and feminine airwoman should look like. Lidyia's crewmembers recalled that she had a bleached white hair and that she always asked them to bring her hydrogen peroxide from the hospital so she could maintain her hair color. She was known not only for being one of the best of the fighter pilots ever but as a person who liked flowers very much.

Rakoblovska told in one of her interviews that becoming a soldier didn't mean that they were supposed to look masculine or act like men. They weren't supposed to undergo some kind of pseudo-male transformation during their training. They stayed girls in many ways but things that mattered the most were their improvement in battle, which was why they worked hard and fought better each day. All of the women from Soviet Aviation groups were different in their attitude and their behavior, but they were all remarkable on the battlefield. They all fought honorably and earned respect from all those who doubted them at the beginning.

The last fight of the Night Witches happened on the 4th of May in 1945 when they flew around Berlin; three days after the Nazi surrendered officially and their final mission was over. Prowse, the historian that researched the phenomenon of the Night Witches said that the German army had their own theories about why "Nachthexen" were so successful in their actions. The first theory was that all of them were criminals and that they all mastered theft. According to this theory, sending them to the frontline was a Soviet punishment for their work against the law. The other theory was one that we already uncovered - the theory of special medicines that gave the Night Witches special abilities and the night vision powers. The fact was that these nocturnal bombers flew more than 800 missions per pilot during the 4 years of war. Their unit alone lost 30 pilots and the total number of missions of Night Witches' (588th Bomber Regiment) was 30,000.

The most controversial thing that happened to one of the most awarded units in the Soviet Union during World War II was disbandment of the unit just six month after Germany officially surrendered and not letting the Night Witches participate in one of the biggest victory day parades as one of the crucial units for defense of the whole country.

# Chapter 6:

# NIGHT WITCHES AND THE LACK OF SOURCES

Until the last few years, there was a limited number of sources that contained the information about the women pilots in general and then about the Night Witches in particular. Soviet Air Forces in their official history books mention that there were females who engaged in combat and participated in specific battles, but they don't mention anything about the existence or formation of all-female air force regiments.

If you take the English translation of "The official history book of Soviet Air Forces" you will find only a footnote that has a short description of the female bombing regiments. The whole book's concept doesn't seem to view the accomplishments of the Night Witches and two other units as something remarkable at the time. Still, some sentences show us the overall impression of Russia towards this topic. The book mentions that

Raskova's units were known as "especially active" during their missions. Also, on some occasions, they showed that they were courageous and had good self-control.

The Soviet scholar named Vera Semonovna Murmantseva was the author who stood out among this limited amount of sources on the topic. She wrote two books and many articles from which the most famous ones were published in Voenno-istorichesky zhurnal and Voprosy istorii. Both of these articles were related to Soviet airwomen and women soldiers in the Soviet Union in general.

In her book named "Soviet Women in the Great Patriotic War" or "Sovetskie zhenschiny v Velikoi Otechestvennoi voine" in Russian, Murmantseva described Soviet women during World War II and their combat engagement. She was one of the first authors that offered statistical data about the number of volunteers for the war and from where they were. She also provided statistics about the number of female casualties during combat. Also, Murmantseva was one of the first who pointed out the significance of legal precedent that Stalin set during the war and the incredible response that the Soviet Air Force got from women willing to fight against the German army.

Even though Murmantseva provided a valuable amount of information about Night Witches and other airwomen in combat, her language was still imprisoned by the period in which she wrote using the patriotic language of that era. However, the data that she gathered represented another kind of important source for this matter. The interesting thing is that the media wasn't blind to Soviet female pilots during the war. At the time, Krasnaya Zvezda" and, Pravda" were Soviet newspapers that published several articles and pictures of female combatants of the country. Additionally, film footage from that period didn't exclude the Night Witches and their two fellow regiments. Still, the most relevant sources about this topic can be found in memoirs, which were written by the surviving members of this all-female highly skilled unit.

One of the most significant memories were "V nebe frontovom" that had two editions. The first one was originally published in 1962 while the second edition was released in 1971. These memories were one of the first real insights into the life of the airwomen that the audience could have. These memories were written with one purpose - to make female accomplishments during the war immortal and to celebrate their achievements along with their fallen comrades. It was written that these memories were dedicated to "The Glorious Memory of Comrades-in-Arms Who Had Fallen While Defending the Homeland."

Kazimiera Cottam, one of the people who translated these memories in English notes said that many of the memories in Russia had mostly just military-patriotic roles and that they were supposed to be understandable and appealing for the younger generation that inherited the country after the war. The goal was to make them aware of the suffering and destruction that everyone faced because of the Nazis and to make sure that the youth would have a view on how to prevent something similar from happening. Yet, according to Cottam, women's memoirs are different because they wanted immortality for all of the achievements that their comrades made, which is why they wrote them in the first place. It was a kind of memento rather than Soviet propaganda. Memoires should serve in making fallen warriors eternal.

Pennington, the historian, noted that these two editions had a big difference between them and that a large number of articles were deleted or added from one edition to another. She also says that the controversy of the chief editor's credibility couldn't be overlooked either. Some veterans doubted the motivation of Militsia Kazarinova, who was the chief editor for both editions. It was doubted that she censored the content, especially when it came to some facts surrounding the female regiments.

Pennington further argued that the Militisia's sister Tamara who was commanding the 856th regiment for only six months, for example, had much more attention than in the first edition and that the work of the other commander of the unit, Aleksandr Gridneve, who held that position for almost three years, was omitted due to the personal interests of the editor. Regardless of the truth behind these changes, the fact is that these memoirs represent one of the most valuable sources when it comes to the Night Witches and female pilot experiences in general.

Some Western countries published articles about the Soviet Union and their female air force units during World War II. Madelin Blizstein was one of the authors who focused on biographies of the most famous pilots of that time and published an article named "How Women Flyers Fight Russia's Air War." In this article, it was possible to find details about Marina Raskova, Polina Osipenko, and Valentina Grizodubova. Still, most of the other sources offered just a list of references for a certain woman or her accomplishments.

Marina Raskova has most entries, and you can find details about her in books such as "The Modern Encyclopedia of Russian and Soviet History" or, Stalin's Eagles: An Illustrated Study of the Soviet Aces of WWII" written by Hans Seidl. Some countries like Korea have entries on Lydia Litvak as one of the world's best fight aces, but neither of these entries offers an insight of the Night Witches and their significance on the battlefront. And sources about the Soviet Air Force that were originally written in English have little to no information about women engaged in air combat. Robert Kilmarx, in his book, states that there were many women in the air force in 1941, but he never elaborated the role that they played while fighting Nazis.

Boris Kuban was a photographer who offered a more visual approach to life when it came to female units in the Soviet Air Force. The importance of the women's role was demonstrated by preferences that varied from the prostitution problem and the brass bands. Kuban focused on the fact that many of these women were disbanded after war regardless of the fact that many of them became war heroes, the Heroes of the Soviet Union nothing less. He talked a lot about this and unintentionally provoked many questions about the demobilization of the Night Witches and other airwomen after the war. The fact was that almost all of the Bombing Regiment members were either dead or disbanded and that only six months after the war finished, there were almost no females left in the air force of the USSR.

Other sources such as Jean Alexander's "Russian Aircraft" or "The Soviet Air Force Since 1918"written by Alexander Boyd mention seven female pilots that had a role in certain battles. Von Hardesty also mentioned them in his book "Red Phoenix: The Rise of Soviet Air Power", but none of the authors really entered the scope of how these female regiments worked. However, it is significant that at least they acknowledged their war contribution. There was even a statistic of awards earned by airwomen in Boyd's book with the suggestion on recently mentioned veteran memoirs.

There are a much larger number of books and articles that can be found about women engaged in World War's II combat in general. But the information is usually limited to being a survey of female pilots and, where possible, their other roles during the battles. Some of the books and articles that examine the role of women in combat and role of women in the Soviet fighting forces are: "Women Aloft" by Valerie Moolman, "Women in Combat: The World War II Experience in the United States, Great Britain, Germany, and the Soviet Union" by D'Ann Campbell's, Selected Papers from the Fourth World Congress for Soviet and East European Studies by Soviet People, "Women in War" by Shelley Saywel and "Soviet Women at War" by John Erickson. All of these sources have a short overview of the formation of the Night Witches and the other two all-female Bombing Regiments, but they barely scratch the surface of issues that female combatants had during the warfare.

Out of all the authors mentioned above, Moolman is the only one that didn't discuss issues of gender equality simply by relying on the context of the Soviet women pilots. Moolman focused on the events that happened before and during the regiment's formation, and she pointed out all of the famous pilots of the time. Saywell, however, gave some kind of rendition of Eastern Front experiences of the Soviet Union's female air force. She used two techniques for information gathering. The first one was classical historical research while the other was the series of interviews that Saywell conducted with a marine, an army nurse, and one of the bomber pilots. She was the first one who focused on the reasons for volunteering in the army and how men accepted them as fellow fighting colleagues.

Erickson had a similar focus in his work, but his sections were leveled contrarily to Saywell's. Rather than giving a personal touch, Erickson had factual and brief listings of the planes that women flew, their regiments, missions and so on. His analysis of this matter revolves around the hypothesis that female combatants had issues with integrating into dominantly male regiments and that there was a lot of loose ends for women here, especially when it came to accommodation, medical care or sanitary agreements.

The most famous English source about the Night Witches is the book written by Bruce Myles. The book is known as "Night Witches: The Untold Story of Soviet Women in Combat. Using interviews that he conducted, Bruce's goal was to recreate the events of the 588th (later46th) Night Bomber Regiment otherwise known as the Nichthexen. Despite the fact that this book was one of the first Western books about the women in the air force, and that it's still one of the best-known ones, this book criticizes the Night Witches and their actions.

Contrarily, a fiction book named "A Dance with Death: Soviet Airwomen in World War II" by Anne Noggle, doesn't focus that much on the work of the Night Witches but at the work and achievements of the "White Rose of Stalingrad'- Lidya Litvak. There is even a rumor questioned in this book as to if Litvak was really transferred to one of the all-male units.

A leading scholar on the subject of Soviet female air regiments, Cottam credited this book for being the first one of the Western attempts that really introduced this topic and its relevance. Still, Cottam pointed out that the book can be misleading and that some details are not accurate. The reason for this is, according to Cottam, Myles' writing that was based on the interviews and interpreters that weren't as relevant as they were supposed to be. Pennington was harder on the critique of Myles' Night Witch book. According to her, the author wasn't familiar enough with his sources from Russia and the interviews that had no context resulted in many errors. Since Pennington also conducted several interviews with veterans, she stated that some reported that Myles' book uses unknown names and that many facts ended up mixed.

One of the interviewed veterans, Polina Gelmand, said that when she saw the book in English, she was shocked. According to her, the names and events differed significantly, and she believed that the book was just a writer's forgery of the Night Witches' fate. In the full review that Pennington wrote about the Night Witches' book, she summarized that the Myles' work could be regarded as nothing more than fiction. She said that it would be worse to think of it as a proper source of Night Witches' missions because there were too many incorrect facts. The scholars argue that this book is nothing more than a series of anecdotes that were romanticized by the author and written to create a feeling of reading a popular novel to the reader. Myles made an effort to enrich his stories with statistics of war. Still, he didn't have any cited sources. This lack of care when it comes to the topic isn't the best showcase to the heroes known as the Night Witches. Still, his intention to tell a story can't be denied.

Another author with a book that became a popular source of the story of Night Witches is Anne Noggle. She wrote the book named " A Dance with Death" intending to examine the life in combat. It turned out that it would be a book about the history of the Soviet female air force units. Noggle conducted many interviews, but many have criticized her methodology. Some argued that her interviews weren't as good as they should have been, that her analysis wasn't structured or deep enough and that she has a significant lack of citations of her sources. Two previously mentioned scholars; Cottam and Pennington had different views on the book. Cottam considered that having a series of interviews without a solid background from history meant that this subject needed a more scholarly approach. On the other side, Pennington noticed that "A Dance with Dead" had inconsistency and that it couldn't really be observed as a relevant historical source. However, Pennington acknowledged the effort of Noggle for the interviews that she has conducted preventing them from being lost forever.

If we talk about the most significant contribution to the studies about the Night Witches and other female combatants, we can say that Cottam was one of the most significant names in that domain. She became intrigued by a female navigator that happened to serve in the Soviet Air Force during World War II. Since Cottam wasn't familiar with the role those female pilots had during the war, she soon started her research, and by the end of 1983, she became the biggest contributor to the Western sources on this subject.

Soviet Airwomen in Combat in World War II was the first book published by Cottam in 1983. This was a first book that had a full history of women's regiments along with the translated memoirs of one navigator and biography of Lily Litvak. The Golden Tressed Soldier was published the same year, and it represented a collection of translated memoirs. When it comes to the Night Witches, this book is important because it contained a chapter on pilots from the 588th Night Bomber Regiment, a.k.a Night Witches. These memoirs, as we already mentioned, were published as two editions. One was originally published in 1962 while the second one appeared in 1971.

The latest book that Cottam published is called "Women in War and Resistance," and it is one of the most complete studies regarding the female Heroes of the Soviet Union. Cottam mentioned many times that her aim wasn't to complete her academic study but to provoke further investigation of the topic. The book Women in War and Resistance, according to its author, had the purpose of becoming a starting point to this investigation. Still, we can say that her translation of memoirs was perhaps the biggest contribution because it provided a good primary source for other researchers. Even Pennington gave credit to her fellow scholar by saying that Cottam was a person who kept looking into this field even if many tried to keep neglecting it.

When it comes to relevant sources about the Night Witched and the latest work on the topic, Pennington's book "Wings, Women, and War: Soviet Airwomen in World War II Combat" is one of a kind. This scholar uses all of the resources that we already mentioned, conducts additional research, along with more interviews and provides us with a complete study of female pilots in the Soviet Air Force to date. Most of the previous relevant books or articles had only rough biographies or different kinds of reports that just confirmed the existence of the all-female units. This time, Pennington researched these topics in detail, and it dealt with female pilots not only before and during the war but also in their postwar period. The difference between this and all other books that have been written on this subject so far is the author's consideration of social

problems that were firstly reason than a conse-
quence of enabling women to engage in combat.
Pennington analyzes this course of events on
overall society in the Soviet Union, especially the
impact that this had on the position of females
in military forces. The objective approach com-
bined with personal experiences from war survivors represents one of the most complete examinations of the topic that was ignored for many
years not only in Russian history but in military
and women's history too.

This book can be viewed as one of the best
sources for looking into this matter. Let's recall
that the Soviet Union was the first country to allow women to engage in combat; thus, they became the first ones who allowed female pilots to
be a part of combat missions. Additionally, World
War II was the first and the last time that women
were allowed to be a part of real combat missions
of that scale. Even though there is a lot of information about the Night Witches and other two
female regiments, it seems like their post-war demobilization erased their effort through the four
glorious female years of history.

As we said, most of both Western and Russian
sources on the Night Witches are still very limited, and they most frequently have a paragraph or
even less to describe the significance of all three
all-female regiments in the Great Patriotic War.

If we had to grade the sources by their value, we would say that the first important ones are the translated memoirs of female airwomen veterans, and later, works of two scholars – Cottam and Pennington who are the main contributors to the contemporary knowledge on brave ladies who terrified the enemy on the frontlines.

# CONCLUSION

As you can see, the Night Witches weren't only a phenomenon that terrified the Nazi armies by their sudden and skillful night attack. They were also brave warriors who achieved becoming the most respected ladies in the whole world. Their leader was a woman who fought her way through the predominately male society and used that influence to form the first all-female military units that could engage in combat. Even though they had to face many hardships, they carried out their missions like no men could do, and many of them became Heroes of the Country.

The 588th Night Bomber Regiment was later named the 46th Guards, but in history, they will stay remembered as the Night Witches- those who harassed Germans during their sleep, who terrorized their camps and dropped more than 23,000 tons of bombs on the German army. The Night Witches were young and motivated. They had to undergo harsh training and work even harder than all other members of the air force just to prove that they can fight alongside their male comrades.

All of these young heroines were volunteers who pledged to give their lives for their home-land, but somehow their legend has faded from the history books. They were the first female pi-lots trained for plane diving, and since they didn't have any high-tech equipment, their navigation-al skills and strategy were impeccable. Still, their battle at the frontline was double-edged because their planes were easily flammable and they didn't have parachutes.

Still, they managed to perform tens of thou-sands maneuvers and fly at least 10 missions each night. The witchy sound of a flying broomstick was a Nazis' way of recognizing the 588th regi-ment since they didn't have any other means to detect them. "Nichthexens" was basically invisible and many of them invincible too.

One of the last surviving members of the Night Witches - Nadezhda Popova - died in 2013. In her interview for the New York Times, she said that her biggest motivation for being a successful pilot with a total number of 852 successfully complet-ed missions was patriotism and on the other hand - revenge. Night Witches became legends among the other members of the Soviet Air Force because of their daring strategy. Their poorly equipped planes always flew in a formation of three. Two of the aircraft were decoys as we already explained, and the third one dropped the bombs.

One of the most relevant factors of the Night Witches' success as the all-female regiment was the cohesion of the unit. This cohesion held them like glue and helped them go through all kinds of adversities along the way. The Night Witches were holding up together surpassing the fear of death and all other unimaginable things that war brought with it.

One of the factors that helped the Night Witches become one of the most feared air combat units during World War II was the aircraft they flew. Their Po2s were defenseless and small, and the regiment had lost many members due to the nature of the planes they had to fly with. Since Po2s were considered to be basically antiquities, the Night Witches soon became the symbol of heroism for women pilots in the USSR. But not only had the Night Witches challenged the rules. Their fellow women bombing regiment - 125th flew the famous Pe2 even though there was a common belief that no women had the skill or strength to fly it.

Finally, regardless of their regiments, all-female pilots had to deal with many different reactions from all sorts of male soldiers. However, the male reaction didn't play a significant role in the cohesion of the Night Witches unit. In fact, after witnessing their skills, most of the men were generally accepting of their female pilot colleagues. Of course, there was an initial mistrust, but, in the end, Night Witches showed everyone that they should be feared and respected. They were one of the pillars of defense against the Nazi occupation and unfortunately almost forgotten in the years that followed.

Hopefully you enjoyed this book and if you found it useful in any way, a review

On Amazon is always appreciated!

Also make sure to follow us at:

Facebook:@History Titans

Twitter:@History Titans

To be notified of FREE new ebook releases!

CPSIA information can be obtained
at www.ICGtesting.com
Printed in the USA
FSHW021616161220
76947FS